PLAY TO LIVE

Brian VanDongen

PLAY TO LIVE
Copyright © 2019 Brian VanDongen
All rights reserved.

Published by BVDPlays 2019
Hillsborough, New Jersey

ISBN 978-1-7329694-1-4 (paperback)
ISBN 978-1-7329694-2-1 (hard cover)
ISBN 978-1-7329694-0-7 (electronic)

bvdplays.com

DISCLAIMER

Play is fun because sometimes it is risky. Sometimes when we play, "it's gonna hurt."

To all those who want to play,
To all those who need to play.

Contents

"We don't stop playing because we grow old; we grow old because we stop playing."

-George Bernard Shaw

"Play energizes us and enlivens us. It eases our burdens. It renews our national sense of optimism and opens us up to new possibilities."

-Stuart Brown, MD

INTRODUCTION:
WHAT IS PLAY?

"Play."

It seems like such an easy word to define. It is used regularly in our daily life.

Consider these two common examples of how we use the word "play."

"My daughter is going to play a soccer game today."

"My son's favorite game, on family game night, is Scattergories."

Most of the time, when we use the word "play", we use it in the sense of a sport, a competition, or a board game. And those are perfectly acceptable and valid uses of the word. It's hard to fault someone who uses "play" to describe the act of participating in a sports or board game.

However, there is so much more to the word.

Stage shows are often called "plays." Actors *play* characters in those shows.

Musicians *play* an instrument.

Graphic designers *play* with colors, shapes, and fonts.

Confused yet? Maybe play is harder to define than we think it is.

The *Merriam-Webster Dictionary* defines "play" (as a noun) as "a recreational activity, especially the spontaneous activity of children." The *Oxford English Dictionary* describes "play" (as a verb) as "engag[ing] in activity for enjoyment and recreation rather than a serious or practical purpose."

Two questions immediately come to my mind after reading those dictionary definitions. One: why is play "especially children"? And two: Is there serious or practical purpose to play?

So maybe, there is a better definition.

We probably know "play" when we see it. And there are certainly characteristics of play that are easily identifiable—ones we can point out when we observe someone at play, or someone playing. Let's look at those.

Play is an activity that is self-initiated and freely-chosen. It requires active involvement and engagement. Play is all about the *person playing*: what he or she does and what he or she *wants* to do. People play because they want to play: play is fun! There are no outside or extrinsic rewards for play; play is always intrinsically motivated.

There are many kinds of play, including physical, social, fantasy or imaginative, constructive, and nature. And this list is by all means not an exhaustive one.

Throughout this book, you will read about different types of play, how different people play, and the benefits they get from playing in their own way. Hopefully, you'll find a story that inspires you, or makes you think of play in a different way—and in *your* own way.

The best thing about this definition of play not defined by the dictionary is that anyone playing cannot play "wrongly". There is no right or wrong way to play. Whatever manner in which that person chooses to play is completely acceptable.

So, perhaps the best definition of play is that "play is in the eye of the player."

HOW TO USE THIS BOOK

Throughout this book, you will read about stories, case studies, and examples of play. At the end of most chapters, there will be a list of tips, ideas, and suggestions, in a section called "Here's the Play." Take those for exactly what they are intended to be: tips, ideas, and suggestions on how to get more play in your life, or in the lives of your loved ones. Because, remember, there is no right way to play and there is no wrong way to play. I'm not going to tell you how you *should* play. After all, play is in the eye of the player.

1

MY YANKEE STADIUM

It was a warm summer afternoon in between my fourth and fifth grade years. I was anxious. Because of school redistricting, I would be going to a new elementary school for only one year, my fifth grade year. In sixth grade, I would change schools again, but I would be attending middle school for my sixth, seventh, and eighth grade years. That made me a little nervous. Two new schools in two years. An entirely new group of kids would be in my fifth grade class. A year later, all the fifth graders from the six other elementary schools in my town would come together for sixth grade, in a school that was nicknamed "the big house." There would be many changes to adapt to, and many new people to meet, over the next two years. The teachers from my old school had told me that there would be benefits to transferring to a new elementary school. They told me that being forced to meet new people, and change my environment, would prepare me for the middle school. I wasn't necessarily buying it.

My neighbor, Tyler, was in the same situation in which I found myself. He was in my grade and we would both be going to the new elementary school. It helped to have a friend.

Ever since my family and I moved into our house, when I was entering first grade, Tyler and I had been best friends. Our dads managed the tee-ball team we played on together when we were six, and then managed our Little League teams every year after that.

We both had younger brothers and were the two oldest kids on the block. Tyler and I considered ourselves the "kings of the neighborhood." Our neighborhood was full of kids, most just one or two years younger than us. We got along well with most of them.

My neighborhood was a typical central New Jersey suburban neighborhood. Our streets had cul-de-sacs. There were drainage retention basins beyond some properties. There was a playground down the street, within walking distance. It seemed at least one parent in every house rode the Raritan Valley train line to their job in Newark or New York City. There were wide streets with sidewalks and street lights. It was idyllic suburbia.

Most afternoons, after the school bus dropped us off at the corner, Tyler and I ran to our houses to discard our backpacks and have a quick snack—after all, we were growing boys! Then, went back outside. We knocked on neighboring doors, asking parents if their kids could come out and play.

Some days, we had more success than others in getting all the kids to play. Regardless of how many kids joined us, though, Tyler and I *always* wanted to play. We shot baskets at our neighbor's driveway basketball hoop, tossed around a football in the stormwater retention area behind my house (sometimes even after a storm, much to our mothers' chagrin), or created obstacle courses on the neighborhood playground. We never had a problem finding something to do.

However, there was something special about those days when we had *all* the kids in the neighborhood playing with us. The warm summer afternoon of this story turned out to be one of those days.

The end of the street I lived on had a cul-de-sac. On days when we had a large group of neighborhood kids with us, that cul-de-sac turned into Yankee Stadium (or, if you were a—gasp—Mets fan, Shea Stadium). With the help of a perfectly placed sewer manhole that was our pitcher's mound, we broke out the sidewalk chalk and drew bases, batters' boxes, and—somewhat crooked, but still effective—foul lines. The outfield wall was the four-inch cobblestone curb—a very hitter-friendly feature. What wasn't so hitter-friendly was the deep straight-away centerfield wall, which was a consequence of the circular configuration of our cul-de-sac (I mean, "stadium") and made it hard to hit homeruns to centerfield. Our stadium had character. Our stadium had charm. It was our stadium.

As self-appointed neighborhood kings, Tyler and I were captains for the two teams. We realized early on that it wouldn't be fair for both of us to be on the same team, for these neighborhood games. After all, were both part of the dynasty—and I'm using that word in the loosest of terms—that was my town's Little League Twins.

The rules evolved as the game was played. After all, "real" baseball rules can only be applied to a cul-de-sac pick-up wiffleball game to a point. For example, nobody wanted to strike out, so we used a cone for a batting tee after too many swings and misses.

In one half-inning, when my team was in the field, we couldn't get anyone out. Tyler's team kept finding the holes in our defense. I think they scored approximately eight runs in that half-inning. I suggested that my team take a turn at bat. How long could I spend in the field, anyway? Hitting is where the glory is. After some discussion, we agreed on a run-limit rule. Tyler (naturally) was not a huge fan of that rule, but I think he realized that if his team was in the same situation, he'd have asked for a run limit, too.

There were two streetlights in that cul-de-sac, and these served as the "stadium lighting". Our stadium never hosted a night game, though—if the lights came on, the game was over. Sometimes "parent" rules take precedence over "kid" rules.

During that warm afternoon, I didn't think about my new school. I didn't think about the fact that I was nervous about that new school. That day helped. I simply *played*.

———

In those days, everyone played—well, at least, the kids did (I didn't really pay attention to what the adults were doing.). The neighborhood of my childhood was full of active, happy, and playful kids.

My parents still live in the same home, in that same neighborhood. Many of the houses remain unchanged. Tyler's house still has the pale-yellow siding it did when we were kids. The playground has the same slide, swings, and sandbox. The neighbors are different, though. The families I grew up with moved out, and new families—with new children—moved in. Even though the neighborhood looks the same, I hardly recognize it today.

Something fundamental has shifted. The sight of cheerful children, playing games in their yards or in the fields; drawing their latest sidewalk-chalk masterpieces on their driveways (only to have them washed away in the next rain storm); or climbing, swinging and sliding on the playground are all but gone.

Gone, too, are the swishing sounds of a perfect shot in the driveway basketball net; the iconic ring of a bell on a bicycle; the laughter of kids as they enjoy being outside.

And another thing—the change that hurts me the most: our baseball stadium in the cul-de-sac sits barren. The chalk-drawn bases and foul lines from my days are obviously long gone. However, there was no indication they had been redrawn recently. The cone we used for a batting tee? Also gone. The extra wiffle balls that lined the curb are missing, too. Two things, however, do remain: the sewer manhole cover and my memories of our cul-de-sac stadium.

This was not the neighborhood I grew up in. How could a neighborhood, with houses so full of children, be so quiet? So empty? So still?

One recent Memorial Day, my parents had a barbeque at their house—my childhood home. Many of our family and friends were there, and it was a good day. At one point, I had to take a walk down the street, to the cul-de-sac. And, when I got there, I stood on the pitcher's mound. I mean, manhole cover. No. *Pitcher's mound*. I closed my eyes. I took a journey back to that summer day, between my fourth and fifth grade year, when I forgot all my problems and all my worries, with the help of that neighborhood wiffleball game. Even though the stadium was empty that day, I still saw the bases and foul lines we drew. I saw myself pitching what I imagined to be a perfect curveball to Tyler, only to also imagine Tyler hitting it anyway and blasting it over the outfield wall (the four-inch-high curb). Even in my imagination, I still couldn't strike him out—after all, his team was the reason we had to put in that run limit! What I saw was my childhood.

I did move off that manhole cover in the middle of the street, after a short while. (My adult self realized that standing in the middle of the street—even if it was a small, quiet cul-de-sac—with my eyes closed wasn't the best idea in the world). On the walk back to my parent's house, it dawned on me. That day, when we played in that stadium, and all those other days when we played, was more than just play.

Play is an experience. Play is a feeling. Play is learning. Play is stress relief. Play is growth. Play is fun.

I decided I couldn't let my Yankee Stadium sit quiet any longer.

I found some sidewalk chalk in my parents' garage—probably left over from when I was younger—and a wiffleball and bat. I gathered the guests together and took the party down to that cul-de-sac. I drew out the bases and foul lines (they still weren't straight). My brother took Tyler's place as a team captain, and he and I selected our teams. This time around, in the hope of preventing any conflict between the players, we settled on the basic rules before the first pitch. If only we'd had this idea all those years ago!

That first pitch came as the sun was setting. After the first inning, the street lights came on. We didn't stop playing. My parents couldn't overrule me, this time. That Memorial Day, my cul-de-sac stadium hosted its first night game. And it was one of the best games in the history of that stadium.

2

WHERE DID PLAY GO?

My story is not uncommon.

When I was a kid, my parents had only one rule: "just be home when the streetlights come on." That's why my cul-de-sac stadium never hosted a night game, when I was young.

Play was liberating. All that was needed to play was a backyard or nearby field, a ball, and other neighborhood friends. Games were made up on the spot, using whatever equipment, field space, and players were available. Play was inclusionary, imaginative, and interesting. Goals were set up using trash cans. The "safe zone" in a game of tag was the dark tube on the playground that everyone was afraid to go into. There had to be *some* risk to the reward of being immune from tagging! Creative hiding places were found all over the park and backyards, because "*Ready or not, here I come!*"

Play was easy. Play was basic. Play was simple.

However, somewhere along the way—and it is hard to pinpoint exactly when—this form of free, liberating play was replaced by organized sports leagues. Recreational programming—for children as young as three years old—became the norm. Highly competitive travel sports teams, for children as young as *seven* years old (or in some cases even *younger!*), became common. Play became formal.

(One small note: I am a recreation professional. I fully believe in, and support, the need for quality recreational programming for everyone. There can be great power in it. I also believe in the need for ample opportunities for unstructured free play time, for everyone.)

The formalization of play has evolved from three root causes. The first is the fear parents feel about their children playing unaccompanied and unsupervised. A second cause is the increase of sedentary behavior at school (mostly due to of a lack of recess time, and fewer physical education classes), and the focus on "measurable and observable" achievement. The final cause for the formalization of play is the professionalization of youth sports. Another common reason cited by parents is a concern for the child's safety.

Strangers Are Not Dangerous

> *"Stranger, if you passing meet me and desire to speak to me, why should you not speak to me? And why should I not speak to you?"*
>
> -Walt Whitman
> *"To You"*

Pauline Reade.

John Kilbride.

Keith Bennett.

Lesley Ann Downey.

Edward Evans.

These are the names of the five children who were sexually assaulted (and, eventually, murdered), in Manchester, England, between 1963 and 1965. They were all between the ages of ten and seventeen.

Ian Brady and Myra Hindley (named by the press as "the most evil woman in Britain"[1]) were both called "sadistic killers" by their sentencing judge. They were known as "the Moors Murderers".

The Moors Murders were the first of an explosion of horrible and atrocious crimes against children, occurring in the United States and England, from the 1960s onwards. These crimes made headlines consistently, in the morning newspapers and on the evening news broadcasts.

A February 1963 edition of *The Austin Daily Herald* advertised the annual Austin, Minnesota Policeman's Ball. The raised funds would support the Policeman's Benevolent Association of the town to finance, among other things, a short film for elementary school students, warning them of child molestation. The film was called "Stranger Danger."

By the 1980s and 1990s, with the advent of television cable news networks, news media had evolved from the traditional morning newspaper to a twenty-four-hour

---

[1] "Hindley: I Wish I Was Hanged" *BBC News, World Edition.* 29 February 2000. Web.

news cycle. These horrific crimes against children were reported on much more frequently. Cable news networks had to fill an entire day with news so, naturally, stories were now repeated and sensationalized. Parents and children could hardly pass by a television without hearing about these crimes.

The twenty-four-hour news cycle that started during that time has evolved into instantaneous, rapidly spreading news. It is available at our fingertips, on the Facebook and Twitter apps on our smart phones. Information is more readily available, today, than at any other time in history. And that information can spread, and become sensationalized, extremely quickly.

Because of the immediate access to news, it makes sense to assume that crime is at an all-time high. However, a University of New Hampshire study (from their Crimes Against Children Research Center) indicated that violence against children ages two to seventeen decreased between 33 and 43 percent, from 2003 to 2011[2].

---

[2] Finkelhor, D., Shattuck, A., Turner, H.A., Hamby, S.L. (2014). "Trends in Children's Exposure to Violence, 2003 to 2011. *JAMA Pediatrics.* http://www.unh.edu/ccrc/pdf/poi130100.pdf

And those strangers who are so dangerous to our children? They are, in most cases, not the ones committing crimes against children. The National Center for Missing and Exploited Children states that most children are abducted by someone they know. And those abduction rates are far lower than perceived. A U.S. Department of Justice report indicated that of the eight hundred thousand children reported missing each year, only one hundred and fifteen are a result of a stranger abducting a child; most are runaway teenagers, who return within twenty-four hours.[3]

In relation to this data, perhaps a YouTube commenter from a "Say No to Strangers" video said it best, when they commented, "We teach our kids about strangers, but it's the ones they know are the people they need to look out for."

Based on these statistics, the world is safer now, for children, than it ever has been. However, because of "stranger danger", children are being robbed of the chance to play and explore the world on their own.

Fearing strangers is no way to go through life. The gas station attendant is a stranger. The server at the

---

[3] http://www.freerangekids.com/crime-statistics/

restaurant is a stranger. The teller at the bank is a stranger. People have to talk to, and rely on, strangers, every day.

Fortunately, there is an effort to rethink "stranger danger", led by Safely Ever After. Safely Ever After is an educational company, whose purpose is to help kids learn "street smarts" (or, in the organization's friendlier parlance, "safe smarts"). Its ten "play-it-safe" rules empower children to harness their own feelings of safety and comfort, and to trust those instincts when something or a situation doesn't feel quite right. Moreover, these ten rules can be taught to a child of any age—even very young children can understand and use them.[4]

No one is suggesting that children—especially young children—should be left entirely on their own, outside, or at a distant playground, or free to roam the neighborhood. The teachings of "safe smarts" aren't about that.

---

[4] Safely Ever After's Super Ten, Play It Safe Rules for Kids and Grown-ups can be accessed at
http://safelyeverafter.com/tenrules.html

Instead of teaching children to "never talk to strangers" and to "stay away from people you don't know," it is crucial to reframe that discussion and let children rely on their own feelings of safety. This can be taught at home and schools. It can be taught through play-acting scenarios and letting children (at a young age and under supervision) talk to or meet strangers. Let the child order his or her own meal, or ask the dog owner at the park what the dog's name is. Simple, small tasks will help children understand their own feelings of safety and comfort in a variety of situations, as well as prepare them for a future of play and life, without constant supervision and direct oversight.

By robbing children of the opportunity to play without close supervision, adults can stifle a child's creativity, sense of wonder, and feelings of self-trust, safety, and comfort. Play is an educational experience for all children; they learn when they play.

School Is Not Just A Classroom

> *"Play gives children a chance to practice what they are learning."*

-Fred Rogers

Play has a crucial role in a child's development and education. School teachers agree. A 2018 survey, conducted by the International Playground Equipment Manufacturers Association (IPEMA) and Voice of Play, revealed that 100% of teachers agree that recess is essential for a child's mental and physical development. They state that, after recess, 81% of teachers report a positive behavior change in students.[5]

If teachers believe this, then it certainly is not translating into policy: only six states—Connecticut, Florida, Indiana, Missouri, Rhode Island, and Virginia—required recess in 2017[6]. This data comes from District Administration, a publication for school district leaders. It is worth noting that both houses of the New Jersey state legislature passed a bill mandating recess for students in Kindergarten to fifth grade. However, the bill was vetoed by Governor Chris Christie in 2017. He called the bill "stupid."

---

[5] Statistics taken from the 2018 Survey on Recess: http://voiceofplay.org/2018-survey-recess/

[6] Blackburn, S. (2017 Oct 25) States That Require Recess, States The Require General Physical Activity. *District Administration.* Retrieved from https://www.districtadministration.com/article/states-require-recess-states-require-general-and-physical-activity

Mandating recess is not "stupid". Recess has the support of the teachers. Recess has the support of elementary school principals, who overwhelmingly agree that recess has a positive impact on both learning in the classroom and student achievement.

(Fortunately, for the young people in New Jersey, Governor Phil Murphy showed his support for compulsory recess in 2018. He signed the bill mandating recess, for all elementary school students in the state.)

So, why is recess limited? Why do only 40 percent of school districts have a recess policy? One answer could be because education is data-driven and focused solely on achievement measures. However, play is not like spelling or multiplication or vocabulary test scores—the benefits of, and knowledge and skills derived from, free play cannot be measured, or marked on a chart indicating growth.

Standardized testing is a major culprit for the lack of free play and physical activity in schools. The results are measurable and, supposedly, statistically valid. Many schools receive funding from their state government, based on their students' performance on these tests.

No Child Left Behind—the most recent revision of the Elementary and Secondary Education Act—was enacted in 2002 and put an emphasis on annual testing for students. Since the enactment of No Child Left Behind, recess time in schools dropped, on average, by fifty minutes. Half of first-graders are scheduled no recess time.

The thinking usually goes something like this: "The more time students are taught the test—and how to take tests—the better they will perform on those tests." The result of that philosophy is a group of children who are physically illiterate and overly anxious, but good at filling in bubbles on a test score sheet. Since school days can only be so long, the time added for academic work and test-taking skills must be taken from somewhere. Sadly, recess and physical education are typically the first areas reduced or eliminated. Since 2001, 20 percent of school districts decreased time for recess and 9 percent decreased time for physical education, in favor of more time for math and science.

The Center for Disease Control and Prevention recommends children receive one hundred and fifty minutes of moderate-to-vigorous physical activity, per week. Most children do not achieve close to this level of physical activity. A 2016 SHAPE America report identified that only five states, and Washington, D.C., require schools to provide physical education to elementary school students, in order to meet the recommended level of weekly physical activity. Only six states require recess daily. This lack of required physical activity and play in schools leads to ultra-structured, rigorous, academic school days, even in elementary schools.

If school is supposed to prepare children for the future, then failing to provide opportunities for children to be physically active, and play, is failing to prepare them.

Physical education classes are not only for the benefit of creating healthy students—although instilling a love for physical activity at a young age should not be overlooked. According to a study by Active Living Research, regular participation in physical activity benefits academic performance. The Institute of Medicine cited more active students are better able to focus on tasks, have better working memories, and score better on standardized tests than less active students[7].

---

[7] *The National Academies* (2013 May 23) Educating the Student Body: Taking Physical Activity and Physical Education to School.

A review article by the Center for Disease Control and Prevention cited that eleven of the fourteen studies they examined found at least one positive relationship between enrolment in physical education classes and higher student academic achievement.

Physical education is not a substitute for recess, nor is recess a substitute for physical education. Both are crucially important.

Physical education teaches people fundamental movement skills and helps them gain physical literacy. Recess lets kids explore, on their own, how to move. Without the confidence in their physical literacy skills, children will be less inclined to move and be physically active at recess.

One in three children are physically illiterate. It is unfair to expect children to be physically active and play on their own, without teaching them the necessary skills. Think about it: children wouldn't be expected to know

---

Retrieved from
http://www.nationalacademies.org/hmd/Reports/2013/Educating
-the-Student-Body-Taking-Physical-Activity-and-Physical-
Education-to-School/Report-Brief052313.aspx

how to solve a word problem in math class without first knowing how to read and how to perform the basic arithmetic needed. So, why are children expected to be confident in their movement—and show a desire to be physically active—if they aren't taught the skills to be physically literate?

Physical activity and play benefits extend far beyond the classroom. If school is supposed to prepare children for life and become well-rounded adults, then children need physical education in school to gain confidence in their physical literacy. Children need recess to have time to be physically active and play.

Play enhances creativity. Play improves social skills, such as communication, negotiation, conflict resolution, and empathy. According to The Genius of Play, a study found that the best predictor of academic performance in eighth grade students was a child's social skills in third grade[8]. In addition, social abilities and creativity are crucial skills in "the real world." The

---

[8] Enhance Social Skills (n.d.) *The Genius of Play.* Retrieved from http://www.thegeniusofplay.org/tgop/benefits/social/genius/benef its-of-play/enhance-social-skills.aspx?hkey=55b354a8-8617-445e-bb1c-b0682417b80b#.XABN0WhKiUk

three R's of academics—reading, writing, and arithmetic—need to become four, to include recess.

Play isn't only *important* to education. Play *is* education.

The value of play and its positive effect on child development is not lost on teachers and principals. In one survey, 100% of teachers said that recess was crucial for children, in both their educational success and personal growth. At the end of the school year at an elementary school in Metuchen, New Jersey, parents ask the principal what they can do with their child over the summer to prepare their child for the next school year. His response is simple: "Play and bake cookies." That is a perfect summer assignment for a child.

A child's school days are highly structured and scheduled. Similarly, the working days of most of their parents are set by a strict timetable. It has almost become "just another chore" to let kids run around and be kids, *without* guidelines or a schedule. It seems easier for adults to schedule and formalize play, so they can fit it in their calendars and make sure that children grow according to objective measures.

Children Are Not Professional Athletes
"Just play. Have fun. Enjoy the game."
-Michael Jordan

Where do parents turn, when seeking avenues for their child to play? Most sign up their child for a youth sport. This is a good thought and the parents' hearts are in the right place: sports do help children learn and develop some of the same life skills that informal play does. However, where these organized activities fall short is in the areas of self-expression, creativity, and imagination. Instead, these programs favor structure and arranged schedules. Children need to develop and refine their motor, and locomotor, skills, prior to seeing significant advancement in sport-specific skills. Most of the time, even though their intentions are good, youth sport coaches (many of whom are volunteers) try to reach too far, too quickly, at too young an age. They attempt to teach children advanced skills related to their sport, before the child is ready to learn them.

Think of a group of baseball players, who play nearly every day (sometimes two games per day, on the weekend) for months, have major corporate sponsorships and a national cable and broadcast television deal. That group isn't just

Major League Baseball players. It also includes Little Leaguers. Every August, children—aged eleven to thirteen—compete in the pinnacle example of the current professionalization of youth sports: The Little League World Series. They are treated, in this series, like Major League Players.

Williamsport, Pennsylvania, is the hub of Little League Baseball. Children, aged eleven and twelve, put on their uniforms, double knot their cleats, and try to get the perfect crease in their cap, in April dreaming of their chance to qualify—through regional and district tournaments—for the Little League World Series in August. It will be their chance to shine, meet players from around the world, and play in front of thousands of fans at Lamade Stadium and Volunteer Stadium— and millions more via a national television audience.

What was once a small, three-team local youth baseball league, founded by Carl Stotz in 1939, has evolved into a mammoth organization with nearly 2.6 million players in the 2008 season (according to Little League International).

Yes, the experience for the teams that make it to the Little League World Series must be incredible. The memories the players make will, undoubtedly, be cherished for their entire lives. However, in a sport and experience that is supposed to be "for the kids", the Little League World Series may not have the kids' best interest at heart. And the adults are to blame.

In 2015, the South Snohomish, Washington, Little League Softball Team intentionally lost. They lost in order to avoid a rematch against a stronger team in the semi-finals of their regional tournament.

The Jackie Robinson Little League team from Chicago, Illinois was a feel-good story of the 2014 Little League World Series. An entirely African-American team, from the southside of Chicago, won the U.S. Championship game. Their story was one that was certainly going to be written into an epic screenplay.

However, after Little League International found that local league officials used players from outside the league boundaries (and were, therefore, rostering and playing ineligible players), the governing body stripped their national title. It still haunts the league today.

Who can forget, also, the 2001 Little League World Series, when pitching phenom Danny Almonte threw the first perfect game in the tournament since 1979? Well, turns out he was too old for the competition. His birth certificate was falsified.

The examples detailed above have nothing to do with the kids. Certainly, these problems are not exclusive to Little League Baseball. They likely exist in every other youth sport. They are all problems created, and advanced, by adults, who may place more importance on the competition than the child participants do. When adults alter the youth sports experience to suit their needs and wants, the kids lose. Cries of "How can you strip away titles and wins from these kids, when they didn't do anything wrong?" are voiced by parents, relatives, and the community.

It is a fair point. It must be a difficult decision to make—whether to penalize the children playing due to the actions of adults. However, these adults make a disgrace of sportsmanship by knowingly breaking rules in order to have an edge in the competition (and, consequently, to bask in the admiration of being the winning manager and league president).

An intense focus on one sport, at an early age, is not beneficial for children. High-level competition for a young child is not appropriate.

The first risk of single-sport specialization is an increased potential for injury. By playing the same sport, day after day, season after season, children are using the same muscles, ligaments, and bones in increasingly repetitive movements. This does not allow for proper recovery time for the muscles to heal and adapt to the training stimulus. Without proper recovery time, injury risk increases.

A study commissioned in 2016 by the National Federation of High Schools (the national governing body for high school sports) found that high school athletes who specialize in one sport are 70% more likely to sustain an injury during the season than athletes who play multiple sports.[9]

Not too long ago, the big concern with drugs in high school sports was performance-enhancing drugs. In

[9] Howard, B. (2016 Dec 20). Injury Rates Higher for Athletes Who Specialize in One Sport. *National Federation of State High School Associations.* Retrieved from
http://www.nfhs.org/articles/injury-rates-higher-for-athletes-who-specialize-in-one-sport/

2005, the New Jersey State Interscholastic Athletic Association (the governing body of high school sports in New Jersey), was the first among the high school state sports associations to implement random steroid, and other performance-enhancing drugs, testing for its athletes. Illinois and Texas implemented[10], and later disbanded[11], drug testing programs for high school athletes.

In the first ten years of testing for steroids and performance-enhancing substances, in New Jersey only three athletes tested positive, and those positives were for banned supplements. Performance-enhancing drugs are not, seemingly, the drugs that athletic administrators, parents, and athletes need to be concerned about.

Injuries require treatment. Of the nearly seven million injuries caused, yearly, by participation in recreational or athletic endeavors, half of them are suffered by people aged five to twenty-four (according to the

---

[10] Griefner, L. (2007 Mar 27) N.J. Steroid Testing Gets Attention in Other States. *Education Week.* Retrieved from http://www.edweek.org/ew/articles/2007/03/28/29steroids.h26.html

[11] http://usatodayhss.com/2016/the-two-states-testing-hs-athletes-for-steroids-turn-up-few-positives

CDC)[12]. Increases in orthopedic surgeries in young people are also evident. Almost half of all "Tommy John surgeries" (reconstruction of a ligament in the elbow) are performed on people aged fifteen to nineteen. While there is nothing wrong with getting injured and needing surgery to fix the injury, it is worth noting how doctors help their patients reduce the pain associated with that injury or surgery.

Most often, doctors prescribe opioids. And opioids are effective in pain reduction—when taken as prescribed by a doctor and only for a short time. However, the opioid addiction in the United States is no secret. With an increase in injuries, more opioids are being prescribed. With the highly addictive drug so readily available, more and more children have access to them. Even if they are not suffering an injury, but have an injured teammate or friend, children have access to the drugs. Unfortunately, the link between opioid addiction and youth sports injury is not so far-fetched.

---

[12] CDC Sports Injuries Fact Sheet:
https://www.cdc.gov/safechild/Fact_Sheets/Sports-Injury-Fact-Sheet-English-a.pdf

A second risk of single-sport specialization among young athletes is an increased potential for burnout. The National Collegiate Athletic Association (the governing body for intercollegiate athletics in the United States) has defined burnout as "the absence of motivation as well as complete mental and physical exhaustion.[13]"

Generally, an increase in competition leads to more extrinsic motivations to play sports (rather than the intrinsic reasons why most children start participating in sports). Extrinsic motivation can only sustain participation for a finite amount of time, leading to burnout. It's hard to blame a ten-year-old for not wanting to play baseball or soccer (or any other sport, for that matter) after having already played hundreds of games and attended hundreds of practices, in his or her young life.

Burnout is a problem because of the benefits participation in sports and physical activity provides. Children who

---

[13] Baugh, C. (n.d.) Preventing Student Athlete Burnout. *The Quad.* Retrieved from
http://thebestschools.org/magazine/student-athlete-burnout-preparing-quit/

specialize in a sport too soon, and drop out of that sport, are less likely to be physically active adults. This result is the exact opposite of a key purpose and mission of youth sports: the acquisition of physical literacy skills to become an active adult and participate in lifelong physical activity.

Adults who participate in sport at a recreational level seem to understand the differences between recreation sport and highly-competitive, professionalized sports. Across the country, social sports organizations are being formed at a rapid pace.

Over two million people participated in a social sport in 2017. What is a "social sport", though?

To some, the ideas of socializing and sport are two separate concepts. However, in the world of social sports, these concepts are intertwined and woven together to form a unique experience for participants looking for both the sporting experience, and the social interaction. These organizations provide a perfect avenue for adults to become active and social.

Social sports organizations are usually open to adults, aged twenty-one years and older. Participants usually sign up for a sport as a team. Some organizations offer individuals the opportunity to register as free agents, and will place them with a team. This gives everyone who wants an opportunity to play that chance.

The following are just a few examples of social sports organizations in the United States.

ZogSports holds social sports leagues in Atlanta, Chicago, Los Angeles, New York, San Francisco, San Jose, and Washington, D.C. Along with the traditional recreational sports, such as basketball and soccer, ZogSports offers leagues in volleyball, kickball, dodgeball, flag football, ultimate frisbee, cornhole and even skee-ball[14].

Beach City Social Sports, in Huntington Beach, California, naturally offers beach volleyball as part of their sports programming[15].

Players Sport and Social Group, in Chicago, brings back the nostalgia of elementary school, with an adult field day, dubbed "Recess with Beer". Teams of between six and eight players participate in mega

---

[14] http://www.zogsports.com/
[15] http://www.beachcitysports.com/

inflatable obstacle courses, human Hungry Hippos, dizzy bat relays, and social media scavenger hunts, to name a few events[16].

The common thread of social sports is the combination of good-natured competition, along with socializing with peers. After the day's games, players in social sports organizations meet at local bars and restaurants—often ones that partner with the league and offer discounts on food and beverages. These post-game happy hours are the perfect time to relive the game-winning three-point shot, the clutch catch on the sideline, the glorious block of a spike, the perfect toss of the beanbag onto the cornhole board, or to have conversation about nothing sports-related at all.

The relaxed nature of these sports put fun and camaraderie above all else. Why do only adults get that opportunity?

Children also need time to decompress, after a sports game. They need to have fun, while playing sports. Their sports should not always be the high-stakes, high-pressure competition so prevalent in youth sports today.

---

[16] http://www.playerssports.net/

"I love watching you play," is the best thing a parent can say to a child on the post-game ride back home.

According to the National Alliance for Youth Sports, 70 percent of children drop out of sport by age thirteen[17]. Over half of youth sports participants specialize in one sport. Of those who specialize, nearly three-quarters specialize before age 10[18]. With this level of participation in one single athletic activity year-round for young children, it is no wonder children are dropping out at alarming rates.

The disappearance of play in childhood affects play and physical activity levels in adults. Children who drop out of sport by age fifteen are twice as less likely to become active adults than those who do not drop out. The competition level, and fun and relaxed atmosphere, that social sports provides for adults seems like a good model to have for youth recreational sport.

---

[17] Dilworth, K. (2015 Feb 11) Would Your Let Your Child Quit A Sport Mid-Season? *National Alliance for Youth Sports.* Retrieved from http://www.nays.org/blog/would-you-let-your-child-quit-a-sport-mid-season/

[18] Russell, W.D. (2014). The Relationship between Youth Sport Specialziation, Reasons for Participation, and Youth Sport Participation Motives: A Retrospective Study. *Journal of Sport Behavior, 37*(3) 286-305.

While there is a time and place for structured sports—even for young children—a primary focus should be on free play. This kind of play has no rules, no expectations, and no formalized outcomes. In its essence, free play is chaotic, but it is also beautiful.

This chapter focused mainly on children and the reasons why children do not get as much free play, and physical activity, as children did in generations past. However, adults are also losing their playfulness, and opportunities to play, due to many of the same factors we see with children: overscheduling, the need for results-driven productivity, and ultra-competitiveness.

In an overly-scheduled, overly-competitive world, play needs to be an escape. Play, by its nature, should not be scheduled or competitive. Play needs to happen organically. Play needs to be accepted. Play needs to happen just for the sake of play.

HERE'S THE PLAY

- Rethink how "stranger danger" is taught to children.
  - Understand that not all strangers are inherently dangerous—children need to learn to speak to strangers, because a large number of daily interactions in adulthood are with strangers.
  - Teach children who "safe adults" are and who to go to if they feel unsafe or uncomfortable in a situation.
  - Allow children the experience of talking with strangers—like the waiter at a restaurant or a dog owner at the dog park—under parental supervision.

- Advocate for the inclusion of recess and physical education as part of a child's school day.
  - Write to the local Board of Education, or attend school meetings, to advocate for recess and physical education.
  - Bolster support for recess and physical education, through school groups such as

Parent-Teacher Associations and local teachers' unions.

- **Allow children to play multiple sports and to find youth sport experiences that are both age and developmentally-appropriate.**
  - Give children the opportunity to play and try multiple sports, even during the same season.
  - Find appropriate programs for the child's age and ability.
  - Ask questions of league administrators to learn their goals for, and vision of, the program, and to gain an understanding of the league.

- **Participate in sport because it is fun.**
  - With social sports organizations being formed all over the country, it is easier than ever to find a sport to play at a recreational level.
  - Competition is a key part of sport and healthy competition has benefits; social sports are a good example of a perfect blend of competition and fun.

- **Play just for the sake of play.**
  - Find playful opportunities in life.

- Play and playful energy is infectious. When someone sees someone else smiling and having a good time, they will likely join in and embrace that behavior.

3

PLAYING INSIDE THE BOX

"In any environment, both the degree of inventiveness and creativity, and the possibility of discovery, are directly proportional the number and kinds of variables in it."

-Simon Nicholson

Architect

Sweet aromas of freshly-baked cookies fill the house. White, powdery snow falls gently from the sky. Wood crackles in the fireplace. At the break of dawn, Katie can't hold her excitement any more. After all, she has been patiently waiting for hours to run down the stairs, to look under the Christmas tree to see if Santa brought her the doll-house she has been asking for all year long. She has been on her best behavior, to make sure she would be on Santa's nice list.

Katie's mom is awake already, creating last-minute touches for that perfect Christmas morning. She sends Katie back upstairs, to wake up the rest of her family. Clearly, this Christmas morning is going to operate on Katie's schedule. Her dad and older brother, yawning and rubbing their eyes, walk down the stairs (at a slightly slower pace than Katie's sprint), to the living room, where the Christmas tree sits, waiting. Katie's mom plugs in the lights, illuminating the tree that always seems to shine just a bit brighter on Christmas morning.

The family tradition—much to the chagrin of Katie's older brother—is that the youngest child opens the first present on Christmas morning. Their mom knew there was the doll house under the tree (and Katie probably guessed that the large box was a doll house), but she made sure that Katie opened that present last.

Katie unwraps the last present of the morning, and her eyes light up. It is the doll house she has been asking for all year long. She is so happy, jumping up and down and running around the house to find her doll so she can play with her beloved new toy. Katie's parents and brother are happy, too, thinking that dollhouse will keep her occupied for hours.

After about ten minutes of playing with the dollhouse, Katie seems more interested in playing with the box the doll house came in. Her mom and dad get frustrated. They saved up their money, in order to buy Katie the toy she wanted all year long and to make this Christmas extra special. And now, she's playing with the box.

Here's the thing, though: it's okay to play with the box.

The box becomes Katie's own doll house, where she can be the princess. Then it became an airplane, where she is a pilot; a race car where she is the driver, and a cave where she is a bear. The box can be anything Katie wants that box to be and Katie can be anything she wants to be.

The great thing about play is that play doesn't require expensive toys or intricate materials. Sometimes, all you need to play is a cardboard box.

A cardboard box is an example of a "loose part". Rocks, water, sand, and logs are others. A loose part is a moveable and adaptable material that can be used for play.

The "loose parts theory" is not new. The term was coined in 1971, by British architect Simon Nicholson.[19] He believed that play with loose parts empowers people's creativity. It's hard to disagree with the theory: a loose part can be anything and everything someone imagines it to be.

Loose parts can be adapted and easily changed. That cardboard box that once contained Katie's dream dollhouse was not just a storage unit for the dollhouse. It became a race car and a cave. Later, it could be a boat. Later still, that same cardboard box might be a spaceship.

Pots and pans can be a drum set one minute and gladiator helmets and shields the next.

A person playing will never bore of a loose part. A loose part can go as far as the player's imagination will let it.

Nicholson believed that creativity was not limited to a select few. He believed that all children were naturally creative, curious about the world, and born to experiment. By having a play environment with many

---

[19] http://ojs.lobo.ac.uk/SDEC/article/view/1204/1171

loose parts, children can experiment, engage, construct, invent, and tinker.

Children don't always play the way adults expect them to. Once a child masters a toy, he or she will quickly lose interest in that toy. A loose part has no specific directions, expected outcome, or desired result. Playing with loose parts is a very pure way to play.

There is no right way or wrong way to play with a loose part: they can be used on their own, or with other loose parts. Bridges, dams, balance boards, and ramps can all be built using loose parts. Sometimes, only the people playing know what they are creating.

Loose parts foster a child's creativity and imagination. They encourage innovation. When a child plays with other children, loose parts support collaboration and teamwork. All of these skills are highly coveted and valued in the adult world.

Adults should introduce loose parts to a child's play environment, while limiting their own intervention into how the child plays. Remember: there is no wrong way to play with a loose part. While adults love to give toys to children and toy companies market their latest and greatest toys to kids, sometimes all Katie needs is to play inside the box.

Katie—and many other children—have the opportunity to play inside the box (and with PVC piping, sand, buckets, boxes, chalk, and plastic containers), at "Loose Parts Play Days" in Baltimore, Maryland. On Friday mornings, in the summer, West Shore Park—next to the Baltimore Visitors Center at the Inner Harbor—is filled with a variety of fun loose parts. Children are left to play—with adult supervision, of course—with virtually no directions, instructions, or goals. What could look like an assortment of trash or recycling ready to be taken away, is actually a collection of materials, meant to be played with.

These Loose Parts Play Days in Baltimore are hosted by a newly formed non-profit organization called "Pure Play Every Day".[20] The organization's goal is to inspire all people who care about children, and the type of adult those children will become, to allow children the freedom to play. They also aim to bring developmentally requisite play opportunities to children.

---

[20] http://www.pureplayeveryday.org

Children are often grouped by age in school, in sports, and in co-curricular and extracurricular activities. While this makes it easy for the adults facilitating the children's experiences, the children's chronological age may not match their biological and psychological needs.

The same is true with play: children's play behaviors are age-related but not age-determined. Children need playful experiences that are engaging, at a level which supports their developmental stage, not their chronological age. Providing loose parts not only facilitates engaging play, but also supports a variety of open-ended play experiences for children. This is what makes loose parts optimal materials for play.

Loose parts help children learn about the world around them, develop fine-motor skills, and acquire and improve body-spatial awareness and sensory systems.

For instance, infant and toddler sensory integration systems build rapidly. At this stage, children need to experience a wide variety of sensory experiences. Young children—much to Mom and Dad's chagrin—find meal time is synonymous with play time. Food from their high-chair tray often finds the floor (and they aren't trying to feed Fido, the family dog).

Why not make mealtime a time for play, though, or at least a time for playful experiences? Giving children a variety of utensils gives them an enriching play experience. For example, a plastic spoon and a wooden spoon offer a child a chance to experience and explore different textures, weights, and colors by feeling and seeing these two different spoons. He or she can also experience speed and sound as a metal spoon falls—or maybe, and more likely, is thrown—to the floor. Look out below, Fido!

The spoon play provides more than just sensory experiences. It also improves motor-skill development assessment. That spoon the child dropped can't just stay on the floor. Mom or Dad will pick it back up and put it back on the high-chair tray. By the parent intentionally placing the spoon on a different side of the high-chair tray each time, the child may begin to reach across the tray with their hand opposite to where the spoon now sits. If the child reaches across the tray with their right hand, to pick up the spoon from the left-hand side of the tray, then that child is beginning to form cross-hemispherical neural connections.

Yes, all of this fun, and learning, can come just from a spoon. Imagine the development and, more importantly, fun, that can come from even more loose parts in a child's world.

As young children mature, they begin to develop their problem-solving skills. This occurs mainly around the preschool age. Loose parts provide an excellent laboratory for children to explore, design, and problem-solve. Plastic containers, like those frequently tossed into the recycling bin (including those that once contained yogurt, sour cream, cut-up fruit, and butter) are perfect loose parts materials. They cover West Shore Park in Baltimore, at the Loose Parts Play Days. However, these containers are hardly trash.

They are materials that children can use for dumping and pouring and provide contextual problem-solving practice. With access to some water, sand, or dirt, children fill, pour, and refill, using the various containers. Numerous scientific concepts can be found in these play-driven experiments: volume, conservation and the relationship between cause and effect.

When a child is too anxious to play with the sand and water and uses all the material very early on, playtime is over. The next time, that child will probably have learned to better conserve his or her materials, so that play time can last even longer. Children can learn scientific principles from this type of play, without fancy science kits. This play can lay the foundation for a lifetime appreciation for STEM (science, technology, engineering, and mathematics), which are increasingly important concepts in today's world.[21]

Play also gives children a chance to form their grasp of ethics. Constant refrains from early elementary school children are protests of "that's not fair" and "that's cheating." These stem from understanding cause and effect. During games, children often have a preformed expectation of a rule. When the result is unexpected, "not fair" exposes their understanding. It feels impossible to go to a playground, or blacktop, or sports field full of young, elementary school students, and not hear a "that's not fair" from a child, at least once. Children need many opportunities to play games and work out fairness, together.

As children progress to the upper elementary school years, they are exploring and practicing effective

---

[21] Stories and information were shared by Patty Stine through email to the author.

communication skills. Loose parts play allows children to create their own games, ones that may not look like any "traditional" game. By giving children inspiration, with materials such as empty plastic bottles, a pair of dice, and colored water, children can create a game and explore communication and negotiation through play. Once children establish an idea, they often discuss and, sometimes, write down the rules. Once the game is tried for the first time, children often refine it, after seeing what worked and what did not. Another round of negotiation ensues. Once it is just right, children will often teach their game to others, because it's so much fun! Games children create on their own are often, in their own words, "the best game ever!"

Loose parts are not only for children. Even adults still find themselves drawn into play with loose parts. This supplies a natural play connection for parents and children, giving both immense benefits. One sunny Friday summer morning, at West Shore Park, a father and his eight-month-old son sat in the sand and constructed an elaborate creation, using a plastic dog food container. The child happily investigated the sand area on his own. Both the father and son found satisfaction and enjoyment during their play. In a different area, PVC pipe and connectors gave a chance for a mom, drawn into play, to help her older son with building a tent playhouse and then a make-believe elevator.

Some of the most famous—and best—toys are essentially loose parts. The National Toy Hall of Fame was established in 1998 in Oregon. In 2002, it moved to Rochester, New York—as part of The Strong, a museum dedicated to the exploration of play—because the Hall of Fame grew too big for its original home.

Toys are inducted into the National Toy Hall of Fame because of their iconic status, longevity, and innovation. In the first nineteen classes of induction from 1998 to 2017, sixty-three toys have been honored. Many of these toys are essentially loose parts.

In the first class, the erector set, frisbee, hula hoop, Lego, Lincoln Logs, and the Tinkertoy were inducted, among others. Sure, the frisbee and a hula hoop have intended uses. However, that frisbee doesn't have to be used only to play frisbee; it could be a plate while pretending to run a restaurant. It could be a flying saucer in outer space.

While many Lego and Lincoln Log kits come with specific instructions on building a certain structure, there is no right or wrong construction with Lego or Lincoln logs. In future classes, the slinky and silly putty have been added to the National Toy Hall of Fame. Even toys as simple as the stick and the ball have been inducted. The recognition of these toys shows that loose parts are an essential component of play.

While the toys inducted into the Hall of Fame are ones that can be purchased, loose parts can be found anywhere. In nature, loose parts are readily available. Sticks, logs, branches, leaves, sand, and water all make for great fun and are perfect examples of loose parts. In addition to their easy accessibility, loose parts found in nature encourage outdoor play. They provide the many benefits of outdoor play and recreation. While it may be cliché, nature often is the best medicine.

In order to keep nature clean—so that everyone can enjoy it—it is imperative, when using parts not found in nature, to choose loose parts that are environmentally friendly. For example, plastics and Styrofoam purchased specifically for the use of loose parts should be avoided. This is because when they are discarded, or not properly stored, at the end of a play day—especially an outdoor play day—they can cause harm to the environment.

In keeping with environmentally friendly loose parts, it is helpful to reuse items. After all, "reduce, reuse, and recycle" is taught to school children at a very young age. There is no reason not to continue to use that mantra into adulthood, when considering play materials.

The cardboard box that Katie's dollhouse came in is being reused as a loose part. Many items used in daily life can be saved and reused as loose parts. An old garbage can, old pots and pans, and leftover PVC piping or wood from home improvement projects are perfect examples. Just as there is no limit to what a loose part can be imagined as, or built into, there is virtually no limit to what can be used a loose part.

Loose parts should have the capacity to be easily manipulated, transported, and used by the person playing. Some loose parts that are too heavy, or awkward, or burdensome for younger children to carry, are not as effective as other loose parts can be. If the child participating in play is not easily able to move and use the loose parts, they will not receive the benefits of loose parts play and may tire quickly—or grow bored or frustrated by the loose parts.

Because there is no right or wrong way to play with loose parts, when playing with, or facilitating, this kind of play, it is best to avoid stifling creativity. Playing with loose parts is largely improvised. Facilitators can use the trusted improvisation technique "yes, and ..." They thus accept the player's interpretation of the loose part, and continue with that line of thought, story, or idea. With "yes, and..." probing during play, communication and cooperation skills are learned and used. Children learn to accept the idea of others, rather than shutting them down, or dismissing them.

Play—and especially play with loose parts—offers everyone an opportunity to build cognitive, social, emotional, and physical skills, throughout their lifetime.

Sure, the new doll house that Katie wanted cost a lot of money. But the box is more fun. Plastic containers, kitchen utensils, sand, water, buckets, and PVC pipe can be too.

The garage of the director of Pure Play Every Day is full of loose parts and probably resembles more of a landfill area than it does a toy store.

And that's okay. Because, sometimes, one person's trash is reused as another person's toy.

HERE'S THE PLAY

- Find loose parts that have no limits to their possibilities and are easy to maneuver.
  - Loose parts that are open-ended and easy to move, build, and play with are more fun, because the possibilities are endless.
  - Choosing light-weight parts makes it easier for younger children to play.

- Use improvisation techniques, such as "yes, and..." when playing with, or facilitating, play with loose parts.
  - The best thing about a loose part is it has no assigned role. What else can that loose part be, when playing? How else can that part be used, to build the structure? What else can you incorporate into your playful scenario?

- These are great types of questions to ask, when playing with loose parts, or observing and facilitating loose parts play with others.

- **Choose loose parts that are environmentally-friendly.**
  - Most loose parts fit the "reuse" aspect of the "reduce, reuse, and recycle" environmentally conscious mantra.
  - When using loose parts to play, try to avoid materials like Styrofoam and plastic straws, which can hurt the environment. (After all, nature is the best medicine, as described in Chapter 7!)

4

RUNNING WITH SCISSORS

"The more risks you allow children to take, the better they learn to take care of themselves."

-Roald Dahl

When the Children's Museum of the Lowcountry[22], in Charleston, South Carolina, opened their new exhibit, people thought they were crazy. They gave kids tools. Real tools. Real saws, real hammers, real nails. They called the exhibit "The Idea Factory".

The Idea Factory started with, well, an idea. The goal was for an exhibit that was interactive—as are so many at the Children's Museum of the Lowcountry—open-end creative, and multi-age. The Idea Factory checked all these boxes.

---

[22] http://explorecml.org/

The exhibit was backed by scientific research. Sawing helps develop gross-motor skills. Holding a screw or nail develops fine-motor skills. Building and constructing projects with no specific directions—or instructions or model—allows children to plan and design, to think critically and problem-solve, and to gain resilience and grit. By using real tools, children acquire real-life experience and become comfortable with tools they will use later in life. Perhaps most importantly, children can gain positive self-esteem by completing projects and using tools, successfully.

The many children who came through the Children's Museum of the Lowcountry experienced those benefits by participating in The Idea Factory.

When the exhibit debuted, there were, naturally, concerns about the safety of the children using these real tools. After all, the only tools most children have experience with are hammers that squeak when they hit something. Fortunately for the museum, exhibits like The Idea Factory had existed at other children's museums, including ones in Pittsburgh, Chicago, and Raleigh. Best practices for this type of experience were already established.

After a meeting of the museum's Parent Advisory Council—who, to say the least, had intense reservations about the Idea Factory when it opened—the exhibit was uninstalled. The advisory group couldn't believe the management put real tools in the hands of children.

What the advisory council says goes, and The Idea Factory was removed from the museum.

A new exhibit was installed, in place of The Idea Factory, called "Hideaways". This new exhibit featured a giant series of children's beds and sheets, which the kids could use to create giant forts—their own "hideaway". This seemed like a perfect new exhibit. Hideaways, like The Idea Factory, allowed children to design, create, and explore their creativity. It was "safer" (although, probably, a better term would be "less risky"). And, kids love forts. The creators of this exhibit anticipated that it would be welcomed by parents, the advisory council, and—most importantly—children.

When Hideaways opened, the first comment from a parent was not about Hideaways, but about The Idea Factory. The comment was this: "I'm so sad to see The Idea Factory go—it was the first time I saw my son, and a lot of children, as growing up. They just seemed older, in a good way. I didn't think he could handle it and then he did. So well. We just miss that space so much."

The mother who provided this feedback is brilliant (also, English is her second language). She isn't afraid of risks. Yet, even she didn't believe her child could do this. However, when her child was able to accomplish using tools successfully, she was elated.

Her comment about her son—and the other children who participated—seeming older, and growing up, was about the competence. The Idea Factory was an opportunity for children to show their caregivers just exactly how competent the children can be. It allowed the children to gain self-confidence, and to experience success with their own competence. It was real testament to how adults in the United States too often diminish the capabilities of children.

The Idea Factory was an exhibit that many people might assume required a constant replenishment of antiseptic wipes and band-aids, maybe even an ambulance stationed outside the museum. However, there were very few injuries. Maybe—somewhat shockingly—no child was injured as they designed and created with real tools. There were injuries suffered at The Idea Factory, however. By parents.

The Idea Factory, at the Children's Museum of the Lowcountry, was a contained, inside area. It had to be, because of the nature of the museum. However, outdoor adventure playgrounds with tools exist around the United States.

On Governor's Island, in New York City, there is an adventure playground called "The Yard". Operated by an organization called play:groundNYC, The Yard boasts a fifty-thousand-square-foot play space equipped with nails, hammers, saws, paint, tires, wood, and fabrics for children—and only children—to build, explore, imagine, and (maybe most fun of all), destroy.[23]

While parents are not allowed in The Yard (there are shaded areas near the space for parents to relax in while their child plays), trained play:groundNYC playworkers supervise, guide, and support the children playing. Open weekend afternoons from May to October, there are three things required for a child to play at The Yard:

---

[23] http://play-ground.nyc/

a desire to have fun, closed-toed, thick-soled shoes, and, of course—in today's litigious society—a waiver signed by a parent or guardian.

Adventure playgrounds, like The Yard, are not an entirely new or revolutionary idea. The concept originated in Europe, after World War II, when Lady Marjory Allen (a landscape architect and children's advocate), studied children playing in the "normal" asphalt and cement playgrounds. She found that children preferred to play by building and creating with parts.

One of the oldest in the country, Adventure Playground was created in 1979, in Berkeley, California's marina. It was ranked as one of the top ten playgrounds in the United States by *National Geographic* magazine. Newsweek ranks it in its top five. Kids design and build forts, boats, and towers, ride zip lines, and paint. With such fun activities such as this, it is no wonder the playground is ranked so highly. Unlike The Yard on Governors Island in New York City, the Adventure Playground in Berkeley encourages parent and adult participation. Signed waivers for all children and adults are still required.[24]

---

[24] http//www.cityofberkeley.info/adventureplayground/

The success of these adventure playgrounds is encouraging others to bring them to their cities. Organizers in Denver, Colorado, are looking to build the "Free Range Playground" to, in their words, "develop the next generation of independent and capable risk-takers through the power of play by bringing unstructured, free-form play-spaces.[25]"

In none of these play-spaces—the Idea Factory in Charleston, The Yard in New York City, Adventure Playground in Berkeley, and the (hopefully established sooner rather than later) Free Range Playground in Denver, is the play unsafe. There is a difference between unsafe, or hazardous, play and risky play.

Unsafe play involves broken or damaged equipment, improper flooring, or a lack of protective padding. Risky play, as adventure playgrounds provide, helps children gain an understanding of risk, allows them to explore their limits, teaches them to make critical decisions, and gives them opportunities to gain self-confidence. It is impossible to childproof the world. Injuries do happen in risky play (although, only for adults in The Idea Factory). The rewards of risky play

---

[25] http://www.freerangeplayground.org/

are too great to warrant avoiding, or eliminating, this type of play. Furthermore, while no one is advocating for anyone to run with scissors, as this chapter is titled—that borders on dangerous, not risky—there are opportunities for children to experience play and create, using real tools, like grown-ups do.

Fortunately for the children of Charleston, South Carolina area, they will soon be able to build, create, and explore. As part of the Children's Museum of the Lowcountry's rehabilitation and capital improvement projects, The Idea Factory will be reinvented, as a new, permanent exhibit: Makerspace. Real tools—and risky play and all the benefits that come with it—will be always be a part of the visitors' experience.

HERE'S THE PLAY

- **Understand the difference between risky play and unsafe (or dangerous) play.**
  - Risky play involves thrill, excitement, and decision-making.
  - Dangerous play usually relates to unsafe play areas.

- Create safe play environments for children to take risks.
  - Play areas need to be kept free of hazards, such as broken glass, loose bolts, and holes or ditches in the surface or flooring.
  - Evaluating risk is a crucial skill as an adult, and can be learned in play.

- Build, create, explore, and destroy—using real tools.
  - Real tools inspire creativity, success, and accomplishment.
  - Using real tools—under supervision—at a young age instills confidence in their usage, and respect for the safety and proper use of them.

5

CLIMBING UP THE SLIDE

"Kids feel powerful scaling the slide. Going up the slide is fun. It's healthy adventure.... Climbing up the slide helps kids test their strength, find their limits and gain balance, spatial awareness, and, yes, social awareness, and consideration."

-Heather Shumaker
Author of *It's OK to Go Up the Slide*

In a bucolic park, in a suburban western New Jersey town, about fifteen minutes from the Delaware River, there are bulldozers, dump trucks, shovels, and a crew wearing hard hats and orange safety vests. An area of the park is full of construction materials, surrounded by yellow caution tape flapping in the wind. Presently, it resembles more of a construction site than the calm, relaxing park the area residents have grown to love and appreciate. However, soon, this park will be blessed with a brand-new playground structure—reminiscent of "old-school" climbing structures—in addition to the two more "contemporary" or "modern" playground structures with slides, ladders, and tunnels, already at the park.

Township officials hope the new playground structure reaches a different age group, and fosters a different type of play. The new climbing structure should encourage more free play, enhance creativity, and allow children to assess and take risks in their play.

Standing next to the site of the playground under construction are two existing playground structures. Just outside the mulch of them, a large green sign is posted, titled "Playground Safety Guidelines." Following the "typical" rules (the playground is open from dawn to dusk, adult supervision is required at all times, pets are not allowed on the playground), each element of the playground is listed, followed by at least two bullet-point rules.

EXERCISE BARS

- Exercise bars should not be used for gymnastics activities.
- No hanging by the back of the knees from the bars.

SWINGS

- Hold on with both hands.
- Stop swinging before getting off.
- Never swing or twist empty seats.
- Do not jump off a moving swing.

SLIDES

- Slide feet first only.
- No running or walking up the slide.
- Do not play under or at the bottom of the slide.
- Do not climb up the slide.
- Do not use the slide as a climbing structure.
- Do not hang feet over the side of the slide.

CLIMBERS AND SLIDE POLES

- No pushing, running, or shoving.
- Play safely and be courteous of others.
- Do not play under or around climbers or slide poles.

If that isn't enough guidelines, above this list is a section titled "CAUTION", featuring additional (what can only be considered) "safety tips."

After reading these decrees, a fair question to ask before playing at this playground would be "so what *can* I do on the playground?" After even a cursory reading of this sign, strict adherence to the recommendations may assume that "fun" is not an option.

If this sign is posted outside the new climbing structure, that would seem to send mixed messages. A new play structure, built for encouraging risky play, would be fronted by a sign that specifically discourages risky play.

This sign was probably created in fear of lawsuits, brought by parents or guardians of children who got injured on the playground. After all, in recent years, people have sued—and, more importantly, won—for less. In a small community, unforeseen legal expenses can wreak havoc on a municipal budget.

Educators, camp counselors, and virtually every other adult involved in organized activities, are all increasingly wary of litigation and poor publicity. Because of this, advice from supervising adults, to kids playing in what is perceived as an unsafe way, is often "Don't do that." Words such as "No" and "Don't", and similar negative phrases, are seen consistently on the sign posted by that playground in New Jersey. However, there is a better way for children to play freely, evaluate risks, and experience success, achievement, pride, and exhilaration, while playing and overcoming their fears. Let them climb up the slide.

When playing, children should largely be in charge of, and determine, their own experiences. After all, the great thing about play is that there is no wrong way to play.

Obstacle course races are full of moderate-to-somewhat-extreme challenges. Swinging from a rope, traversing a see-saw, crawling under barbed wire, throwing spears, jumping off cliffs, squeezing through pipes, and running through electrically-charged wires are all common obstacles at these races. Another staple impediment? Running up a half-pipe, which is virtually no different from running up a slide.

Why is that challenge so accepted at an obstacle course race for adults, but so frowned-upon at a playground for children? What are the differences between the two? Obstacle course participants pay large sums of money to participate in these races; playground access is free. Signed waivers are required to participate in an obstacle course race; there are no legal requirements to go on a playground. Travel to distant or remote areas is required for obstacle course races; the playground is often right around the corner.

The rise of the obstacle course race is astonishing. According to Running USA, the number of obstacle course race finishers increased nearly 1,500%, from 2010 to 2013.[26] From what is viewed as the first obstacle course race—"The Tough Guy", in 1987—to now, the number of participants in these obstacle course races has increased every year. There was one race in 1987: The Tough Guy, in London, England. Now, there are dozens of companies, running hundreds of races across the globe. A quick search of active.com lists no less than two thousand races, from Carlsbad, California to Derbyshire, England and from Blaine, Minnesota to Vega Baja, Puerto Rico. Obstacle course races are popular around the world.

---

[26] Schuckles, E. (n.d.) The Rise of Obstacle Course Races. *Active.* Retrieved from http://www.active.com/running/articles/the-rise-of-obstacle-course-races

Adults are willing to pay large sums of money to put themselves in challenging situations and risk injury. Playing into the extreme challenge of the event, "Tough Mudder" calls their legal waivers "Death Waivers." Of course, participants don't expect to die while on the course. Neither do adults expect children to die, while playing on the playground. Adults take the risk of meeting demanding challenges and achieving success on the obstacle course, but are largely unwilling to let their children experience the same feelings on a playground.

This is not to say that children do not engage in risky play. It is also not to say that playworkers and adults who let children engage in risky play are not fearful of certain play activities. It certainly takes time for adults to adjust their limit of fears as children test theirs in play.

The Bernheim Arboretum and Research Forest encompasses over fifteen thousand acres in Kentucky and, as their website puts it, "is an adventure for everyone.[27]" Over forty miles of trails take hikers and bikers over scenic knobs, through beautiful valleys, and along bucolic ridges and hollows.

---

[27] http://bernheim.org/

There are plenty of opportunities to learn at Bernheim, as well. From large annual festivals, such as BloomFest in May, BugFest each September, and ColorFest in October, to hands-on "ECO Kids" classes (the ECO stands for Every Child Outside) and "lunch and learns", education about the outdoors is not in short supply at the arboretum.

Simply providing a place to play in nature, and offering outdoor education classes, is not enough for the people at Bernheim. An initiative of the Bernheim Arboretum and Research Forest is the "Children at Play Network." Through the Children at Play Network, free play opportunities are created often in order for children to connect with nature. Through these opportunities, the Children at Play Network believes that, as children are allowed to freely explore play in the outdoors, they are building the connections that are the underpinnings of fostering a life-long love of nature. Additionally, if children are allowed to simply play, they often show tremendous curiosity and skill. Often, once adults step into the mix and direct that play, even with the best of intentions, they usually squash both of those beliefs.

Every adult and playworker has their own fears. Some are fearful of children playing at heights. Others are scared of children near fire. Others, still, don't like children playing near water. It's normal for adult playworkers to have fears of children playing. Even Claude Stephens, of the Bernheim Arboretum and Research Forest, has his fears and nervousness, when children play, and he helped create the Children at Play Network.

Ropes are, as he puts it, his "tension point." He is comfortable with children climbing high in a tree or building a fire, but rope play makes him anxious. To address his fear, Claude is very intentional on how rope is introduced into a play situation. However, despite his worries, he does not shy away from rope play, because he knows how much ropes can add to a play environment.

During one very long play day at Bernheim, Claude was observing a young boy, who was probably about seven years old, and how that boy developed a new appreciation for rope. When this young boy first came to the play day, he was barely able to untangle a rope. When the play day ended, the boy was able to build an incredible fort from a tangle of sticks, ropes, tarps, boards, bales of straw, tape and cardboard. Claude provides only short lengths of rope to children who are new to rope. In his experience, long ropes just get in the way of allowing the children to accomplish what they want to do.

At one point during the child's play and discovery with rope, he climbed a tree to tie a rope as high as he could in order to hoist a bucket of building materials. Seeing that rope go up that tree with a beginner rope-user made Claude nervous. However, he stepped back, took a deep breath and allowed the work to progress under his watchful eye. Claude tried to hide his nervousness as best he could, in order to allow the child to build and play. And the reward for that paid off royally. The young boy was so proud of his accomplishment, in building the fort. His pride was even greater when he eventually showed off his work to his mother.

Because Claude resisted an urge to step forward, the child was able to play on his own, build an amazing fort, and have a great sense of pride in his achievement. Would the child have had the experience he did, if Claude had interjected with a warning to "be careful"? The pride he did? The fun he did? Probably not.

"Be careful" is a common warning parents and other adults give to children, when they play in "dangerous" ways. It may calm the adult's fear, but it lessens the child's opportunity to explore his or her own limits.

However, the instinctive, or reactive, "be careful" warning is hardly helpful. This statement is usually said because adults do not want children to get hurt. Risky play is not the same as dangerous or unsafe play.

Children engage in risky physical activity at a very young age. Learning how to walk is risky. Walking is a highly important locomotor skill. Learning how to walk, however, is riddled with falls resulting in scrapes, bumps, and bruises. Yet, when a child learns how to walk, his or her parents are not constantly telling him or her to "be careful."

A child learning how to walk does not know what "careful" is. He or she is learning how to move, learning about the space around him or herself, and how to control his or her own body. That child is gaining confidence in his or her abilities. Even after a fall, a child learning how to walk usually gets right back up and tries again.

A few years later, that child is going to learn how to ride a bike. When he or she is learning how to ride a bike, there will certainly be falls. He or she will also start with a bicycle with training wheels. Then, Mom or Dad will hold the bike as the child learns balance *without* training wheels. Because this fall comes from a higher height (among other reasons), the bike-riding learning child wears a helmet. Sometimes, he or she will wear elbow or knee pads as well. There will still be falls and, potentially, injuries. Still, adults usually never say "be careful" to a child learning how to ride a bike.

Learning how to walk and ride a bike are risky activities, but taken under safe conditions. There is nothing inherently dangerous about learning how to walk that requires extreme carefulness. So why do adults treat most play activities with more carefulness?

A child hanging upside down from the monkey bars will probably be told to "be careful" or to even stop. A child walking across a stream on slippery rocks will probably be told to "be careful." What if, instead of using this phrase, adults supported the child's exploration of risk with better questions?

There are ways to reframe carefulness to get the child to still engage in risky behavior, while evaluating that risk into his or her own comfort level.

That child hanging upside down on the monkey bars could be asked, "How do you feel hanging upside down?"

That child walking across the wet rocks in the stream could be asked, "Are those rocks slippery?" or "What is the best way to cross this river?"

These questions can help the child evaluate his or her own situation, engage in risk, and feel proud of his or her own accomplishments and victory over risk.

Evaluating risk is a key skill in life. By engaging in risky play, children have the opportunity to evaluate risk on their own terms, and can transfer that skill to their personal and professional life, as they become adults.

Those Tough Mudders, Spartan Races, Rugged Maniacs, and every other mud run and obstacle course race around the world, thrive on participants engaging in risky play and risky physical activity. While they all require release of liability waivers to participate, participants are not engaging in any dangerous behavior. And they are fun place to play.

Adults engage in that risky play and risky physical activity in those situations. They pay—sometimes hefty—entry fees, in order to do so!

Recently, those race companies are expanding their business model to include kid races—for entry fees. Adults pay for children to engage in risky play at those events. Once the starting gun goes off, there are no adults telling those children to be careful. They are having fun, exploring risky play. They are running up mini half pipe walls, climbing cargo nets, jumping into pools of mud, just like their parents are on the big obstacle course race course.

The playground isn't any different. Fun play is risky. Risky play may hurt. However, the achievement of climbing up the slide, or hanging upside down from the monkey bars, teaches children skills that last a lifetime. Plus, it's free at a playground.

HERE'S THE PLAY

- Climb up the slide.
  - Climbing up the slide builds strength, balance, and body-spatial awareness skills.
  - Fun and exhilarating obstacle course races can be created on the fly at parks and playgrounds, with a little imagination.

- Be careful saying "be careful."
  - While comforting, saying "be careful" can be a hindrance to play, development of risk evaluation, and self-confidence.
  - Change "be careful" to questions that inspire critical thinking and evaluation, and inspire self-confidence.

6

NATURE IS THE BEST MEDICINE

"In every walk with nature, one receives far more than he seeks."

-John Muir
"The Father of National Parks"

In the parks and recreation world, recreational pursuits and park areas can be described in two ways: active and passive. The term "passive recreation area" is a frustrating one and it isn't one that is intuitive in meaning. To explain, common "passive recreational" endeavors include wildlife observation, walking, biking, snowshoeing, and canoeing, and a "passive recreation area" is typically defined as undeveloped space or an environmentally sensitive area.

Some additional examples of some common "passive" recreation pursuits include:

- Walking and jogging
- Hiking
- Kayaking
- Cross-country skiing
- Kite flying

An argument can be made that these so-called "passive pursuits" *are actually* "active". The term "passive" seems to diminish the quality of the activity, especially when these activities are being done outside and in nature.

In today's increasingly sedentary world, people need to be active. Humans are born to move. Promoting these types of activities as "active pursuits", and legitimate ways to accumulate the necessary and recommended amount of physical activity per day, may help people to get more active and use these passive recreation areas more often.

Because of the nature of these passive recreation areas, many of them are wooded, or rural. People see pictures of these places on the internet and wish they can be immersed in them.

While an overwhelming majority of the American population live in urban or suburban areas—and cannot easily access a traditional forest—green space in urban areas (such as gardens, small "pocket" parks, and street trees) can provide the necessary interaction with nature that humans need.

In recent urban and city planning, the need for green space and parkland has not gone unnoticed. Cities have incorporated green space for their residents and visitors in unique and creative ways.

In 2009, the first phase of the High Line opened in New York City on an abandoned railroad spur in western Manhattan. After additions and expansions, the High Line now runs from Gansevoort Street (three blocks below 14th Street) to 34th Street, passing the Chelsea Market and the Meatpacking District and is near the Javits Center. With gardens, lawns, water features, and walking paths its entire length, the High Line attracts millions of visitors annually and serves a model for creative repurposing of areas into green space, especially in urban cities.

Because of this success, the advocacy group, Friends of the High Line, launched the High Line Network to assist with similar projects in other cities, such as

Atlanta, Dallas, Los Angeles, San Francisco, and Toronto. The creative addition of green space to cities ensures those residents and visitors benefit from the goodness of nature even in their concrete jungles.

———

Nestled in the heart of one of London, Ontario's oldest heritage buildings, the Wortley YMCA child care center has attracted attention for both its interior and exterior beauty. It is one of the largest branches of the YMCA of Western Ontario, with over a hundred children registered in the child care program. The Wortley YMCA center is a true example of embracing natural outdoor landscapes, within an urban community.

A carefully designed intentional balance exists between open spaces and natural equipment structures, at the Wortley YMCA. This balance helps to support learning, across the developmental domains.

In the playscapes, different areas for each age group are divided by garden boxes, which are filled with vegetables, various plants, and the occasional weed. These garden boxes are all cared for by the children enrolled in the child care.

On either side of these garden box dividers, natural structures are located throughout the space, including wooden stages for performances, a sand box for sensory needs, toadstool stumps for group gatherings, and a wide bike path. The open spaces are filled with loose parts, which are ready to be manipulated into the next spaceship, obstacle course, or whatever else the child can imagine.

The YMCA of Western Ontario has a growing and important vision of connecting children back to nature. In 2015, "ParticipACTION"—a Canadian non-profit organization, whose primary mission is to get people to move more and sit less—stated that "the biggest risk is keeping kids indoors.[28]"

Similar to a vast majority of Americans not meeting federal physical activity guidelines, an alarmingly low percentage of Canadian youth and children meet Canada's "Physical Activity and Sedentary Behaviour Guidelines".

When the children play at the Wortley YMCA, the playworkers trust the children to test their limits. They

---

[28] http://benefitshub.ca/entry/the-biggest-risk-is-keeping-kids-indoors/

let the children decide when they are ready to take the next step. By letting the children make their own decisions, through playing, children learn self-regulation, develop resiliency, problem-solve, work together, and practice developing empathy. They do what feels right and decide what to do next.

One parent, whose children were part of the child care program at the Wortley YMCA, and who played in nature, said "changing my outlook has helped me understand children's development and abilities. I can 'see' things differently and it has broadened my imagination. This project has changed how I behave with children outdoors."

Canadians love and appreciate their beautiful natural surroundings. In Canada, it is never too cold to explore nature—there are only wrong types of clothes.

———

Spending time in nature is good for the mind. Humans need to spend time outdoors. In today's fast-paced society, spending time outside helps people focus, have a rest from hectic work schedules, and refresh and renew our brains by taking a cognitive break. Stress reduction and mood improvement are two other key benefits of spending time outside. In 2006, Duke researchers found that walking outside briskly for thirty minutes, three times per week, was more effective for treatment of depression than medication or a combination of medication and walking.

Spending time outside is good for the body. Exposure to forests and nature boosts the immune system. A United States Department of Agriculture report indicated that people who spend as little as fifteen minutes per day outside have fewer diseases, are less likely to get cancer, have a lower risk of heart attack and stroke, and have better bone density. Even better is spending physically active time—including participating in passive recreation activities, such as walking, hiking, or canoeing—for cardiovascular, muscular strength and endurance, and bone density benefits.

Japan's Ministry of Agriculture, Forestry, and Fisheries, in 1982, coined the term *"Shinrin-yoku"*, or "forest bathing"—short, leisurely trips to a forest. In 2009, a Japanese study included a group of men and women staying in the forest for a three-day trip, including light walks each day. Researchers analyzed blood and urine samples collected from participants, and deduced that the results may indicate that nature walks may help in the prevention of cancer.

In an effort to encourage people to go outside for the health benefits, and recognize the positive effects nature can have on some chronic diseases, "Park Rx America" encourages doctors to prescribe nature and visits to parks to "decrease the burden of chronic disease, increase health and happiness, and foster environmental stewardship."

Since April 2018, over one hundred doctors have written over seven hundred prescriptions for park visits, in seven states and the District of Columbia. This number is growing, as the public land stewards and park professionals input their park data into the national database. If just looking at a picture of nature can provide some health benefits, imagine the health benefits of physically being *in* nature.

Nature is one of the best places to play. Play in nature is crucially important. Play is impossibly fun. Best of all, play in nature is easy. Climbing a tree, balancing on a log, hopping from rock to rock, skipping a rock across the pond ... By playing in nature, creativity is boosted and problem-solving skills are improved. Play in nature, even play as simple as this, has many benefits for both children and adults.

Passive recreation areas look—and are—peaceful, calm, serene, and beautiful. However, that doesn't mean that they shouldn't be used for activity!

HERE'S THE PLAY

- Spend time in nature or green space, every day.
  - Just looking a picture of nature and natural places can decrease stress—imagine what actually spending time in nature can do.
  - Doctors are prescribing park visits for some chronic diseases. Nature and physical activity outdoors can also function as preventative medicine, by reducing stress, lowering blood pressure, and improve bone density.
  - Nature can be hard to find in some areas, especially large cities. However, many cities are full of small pocket parks or green space areas. Seek them out. Explore them.

- **Play in the mud.**
  - Gain a connection to nature, and an appreciation for the environment.
  - The mud will wash off, the memories won't.

7

PLAY IS SERIOUS

"It's a happy talent to know how to play."
-Ralph Waldo Emerson

Play is serious. I hope that, throughout your time reading this book, you can come to the same conclusion. Before reading this book, perhaps you thought: How can play be serious? Isn't play just play? Now, you have answers to those questions.

Play is a universal language. Play should be simple. Play should be easy. However, in today's fast-paced, high-pressure world, things aren't always as easy as they should be. Often, people need reasons why we should be doing things, data to back up and prove those reasons, and the time, energy, and commitment to do those things. Play is one of those things we should invest in for ourselves, and for our children. It's time to get serious about play.

Everyone can play. That's right: everyone. Regardless of age or ability, everyone can play. Play can be as complicated or as simple as the participants want it to be. Large-scale games can have elaborate rules and small-scale activities can be drawing on the driveway with sidewalk chalk. Anyone with a desire to have fun doing a self-chosen activity, at their own pace—with or without others—is probably playing.

You can't get play wrong. There is no right or wrong way to play. The only limits are the limits of the players' imaginations. Especially with children, play can enhance their creativity and let the children play however they envision to be fun and fair, without strict adult guidance. Play can be relaxed in nature, or it can be vigorous and planned. There can be specialized equipment, designed specifically for a game, or there can be loose parts—materials with no specific set of directions on their use. These might include twigs, refrigerator boxes, cups, fabric, or even mud (to name only a few).

There doesn't need to be an end goal for play. Often, when people think of play, they think there must be a result. For example, when someone "plays" a sport, there is a winner and loser. The goal is to get more runs, goals, or points, than another player or team. When we play chess, the end is when the opponent has no moves remaining. However, most of the time, there is no formalized goal in play, except to have fun.

Play makes people healthy. The obesity epidemic in the United States is no secret. The majority of children and adults do not get the recommended level of physical activity each day. By engaging in most types of play, children and adults can reach their physical activity recommendation, each day. Physically active play helps children build strong bones and muscles, and reduces the risk of chronic diseases and developing obesity. Adults can benefit from physically active play too: lower blood pressure, lower resting heart rate, strengthened bones reducing the risk of osteoporosis, and preservation of muscle mass, are all key benefits for adults.

In addition to physical health, play also helps promote mental and emotional health, in both children and adults. Everyone—children and adults, alike—are subject to high-pressure situations, regularly, whether at school or at work. While many situations provide high levels of stress in our daily lives, play can help manage stress, and physical activity and play can help reduce depression and anxiety. Play also helps children gain cognitive skills, while, at the same time delays mental decline in older adults.

Play makes you happy. Play helps boost our self-esteem. Play helps children make new friends and learn how to be friends. At its core, play is boundless, limitless, and endless, and play can extend to any stretch of our imaginations. When we are just exploring without goals, without rules, without pressure, we are having fun. And that is what makes us human. We've all heard the saying, "All work and no play makes you a dull boy". We need play to make us happy.

Ralph Waldo Emerson's quote, at the beginning of this chapter, is an interesting one. Is play a talent? Or is play inherent, inside of us? Maybe that talent of play has been diminishing for a variety of reasons; hectic, stressful schedules; a data and results-driven society; more intense competition in sports—especially youth sports—and a potentially negative stigma attached to play for the sake of play might be among these reasons.

However, play is serious. Play for the sake of play is serious. While the benefits of play cannot be measured or identified in one child, like test scores can be—or the impact of an advertising campaign in the business world can be—taken holistically, it is clear that play improves the lives of everyone who engages in it.

In order for the seriousness of play to benefit our life, we need to be less serious. Play for the sake of play is okay, totally acceptable, and definitely needed. There does not need to be a winner or loser in play. There does not need to be measurable data in play. What there does need to be is fun, laughter, imagination, and smiles.

The talent to play is inside everyone. And it certainly is a happy one to have.

HERE'S THE PLAY

- (Read the Epilogue.) Put this book down. Get up. Go play.
  - Be silly, be goofy, be carefree.
  - Jump in the mud, go down the slide headfirst, play with the box.
  - There is no wrong way to play.

EPILOGUE:
WHY I WROTE THIS BOOK

Play is important to me. Play should be, and needs to be, important to you too. That, in essence, is why I wrote this book.

Why is play important to me?

I am a recreation professional and with that comes a whole host of varying duties, responsibilities, and tasks. When people think of recreation departments, the immediate thought is "youth sports". And, yes, that is a key aspect of recreational programming, in most municipalities. However, good, quality recreation departments are much more than just organizations that provide opportunities for children to play sports.

Recreation departments should provide, among other things, summer camps for children, sport classes and clinics, art programs, theater programs, and nature programs. What also must be offered is opportunities for play.

Working in recreation, I've seen the trends—in both children and adults—regarding physical activity and playfulness. And, as I mentioned in Chapter Two, I think play is disappearing. My view on the state of play is rather pessimistic, I guess you could say. While play will never fully disappear—after all, it is part of human nature—it is imperative that opportunities to play and be playful are not reduced or eliminated from our daily lives. While I'm fairly young (or, at least, people tell me I am—sometimes, I beg to differ) at age thirty at the time of writing this book and sharing my thoughts with you, I've seen generations shift in their attitudes toward, and acceptance of, play, in both my line of work and in my own life as a playful person.

People are interesting creatures. We crave structure and organization. We like schedules and routines. However, we also desire fun, laughter, movement, and playfulness. Because of this, we get conflicted. True play is unstructured and unorganized, and not scheduled and not routine. Unfortunately, the structured side of our personality often wins out.

In the first chapter, I told you a story about my childhood which, while slightly romanticized, is probably very relatable to you. Whenever we think of playful memories, we often think of the times we were outside, left to our own free will and ambitions (within reason, of course) by our parents. Those times were the most fun to us. Now, that type of play is hardly seen in children. Neighborhood streets and green spaces are empty, when they used to be full of kids playing. That doesn't happen in today's society, where structure and schedule win out.

Adults have it even worse. If an adult hangs from the monkey bars, slides down (or climbs up) the slide, balances on the curb, or builds a sand castle, that is frowned upon. "It's time to grow up," is a common refrain. It is possible to grow up and still play.

Maybe we just need permission to play. Permission to "act like a kid." Permission to be spontaneous, to be physically active, to be imaginative, to be playful.

You need to be playful.

That is why I wrote this book. I want to help you incorporate play into your life, your child's life, your family's life, and your friend's life. I want you to be more playful.

Play is not just important to education; play *is* education.

Play is not just important to a healthy lifestyle; play *is* a healthy lifestyle.

Play is not just important to life skills; play *is* a life skill.

That is why play is important to me. And that is why play should be important to you too.

So, go find Tyler, or whoever your neighborhood friend is. Or your child, or your spouse, or whoever else. Play wiffleball in the cul-de-sac. Draw with sidewalk chalk. Build with loose parts. Climb up the slide. Get outside and climb a tree.

You have my permission: Be playful.